i lost a poem

i lost a poem

mzwandile matiwana

DEEP SOUTH 2004

isbn: 0-9584542-9-9

deep south
p.o. box 6082
grahamstown
6140
www.deepsouth.co.za
contact@deepsouth.co.za

We gratefully acknowledge financial assistance for publishing this book from
The East Cape Provincial Arts and Culture Council,
The Roy Joseph Cotton Poetry Trust,
and The Cape Tercentenary Foundation

Earlier versions of these poems have appeared in Kotaz, New Coin, Timbila,
Botsotso, Fidelities, Carapace, www.donga.co.za, southern rain poetry,
Writing from Here, and Sweet.

deep south titles are distributed by
University of Natal Press
www.unpress.co.za
books@nu.ac.za

Cover linocut : Shepherd Xego
Cover and text design : Paul Wessels

To my ex-teacher
Miss Buyelwa Sonjica

The greatest education
is to glorify God

Rumi

If the iron is blunt and one does not whet the
edge, then more strength must be exerted; but
wisdom helps one to succeed.

Ecclesiastes 10,10

contents

Our Pride

Our pride is caught in poverty
like an innocent drowning in an ocean
of incest shades

There should be no reason
for violence
to hold down this earth
in the mud of our crimes

There should be no reason my brother, my sister
to denounce peace with our ugliness

Centuries old vomit

For how long must I tell
how quicker and slyer than a lizard
is the lover's eye?

For how long must I tell
of relaxation,
of the eyelids of a pauper?

For how long
must I tell of an infant that sucks
empty and lifeless breasts?

Do I have to take a turn
around the village
and shout?

My ribs are marked
by some great absentminded size ten boots –
do I have to?

Since I was forced to live
through a bad spell
washing the dirtiest washing –

Certainly my friend
I will
I will not sleep beside this vomit.

Count-down

The clock tick-tocked
at the charge office
as if challenging this new climate
there were clippings and clickings
screaming everywhere –
I was a "catch"
so said the chief of staff
who caught me

This new civilisation charmed
and scared me as well –
the clothes
the crew-cuts
The clinical cleanliness
constructed a clear picture –
that I was conquered.

Conscious of these climes
I felt like a cockroach
inside a chilling freezer
and they seemed to celebrate
with their cruel chuckles
that fanned coals of anger in me

My conscience communicated
with my inner certitude
checking the cause
or perhaps what was my crime –
It was like I just woke from a coma

I started to calculate seconds
on that cold cement floor

cuffed hands and feet
Until I became content

I had clots of blood on my face
courtesy of their kicks and klaps
but I chose not to cry

And that courage conquered my captors
I heard a thunder-clap like of their crumbling down

For they could not crack a comrade kid.

That's what I have become

a monster preying on the
present
with the claws of terror
leaving no chance for survival
turned on
by greed
only to be paid with regret
that's what I have become –

a nobody who has
turned
into igongqongqo
with potential to breed scars
and feed hearts with painful wounds –
an izim
boiling the pot of human flesh –
that's what I have become.

Virgin

Tonight is our first night
of countless silent kisses –

I cannot help saying it
Today is Sunday –
I hope you will not make me suffer
when I cross your river

This boat rows only confusion:
I am afraid
For I have nothing to give
But my self

Will you bear with me
and treat me tenderly?

My poems

Branches bowed
by incessant wind
Then there was
a silence.

And before there were strings
that were strummed
And hips gyrated
in an obscene manner
Then there was
a silence.

And before there were written notes
that wafted from my mind
through to the forest
seeking political asylum
another traditional belief
chained in the island
Then there was
a silence.

And before there was a pen and paper
with a head full of notions,
offered in verse and quelled
until a mighty crescendo, it was felled
and left...
Then there were my poems.

Sounds of the sun

Come what may
seasons of love change
as winters come and cross
the atmosphere of smiling misery –
yet still love takes loneliness of the lonely

Beyond the warmth of the blue living skies
confusion swells like the sounds of the sun
ringing the serenity of hopefulness
flowing so slow like the rivers
laying down the dust of sadness

Questions for Kgositsile

My grandfather's voice was a horn
that trumpeted
the slow sadness of my dying
before I could live –

Now I have become a thick and white
saliva
from the dry mouth of hunger –
and the laughter of my teeth
is the colour of shame –
"To be white is holy" so I was told
But how
when hunger is a sin?

Celebrant hear this generation ask:
Poet of music old tell me –
will it be a sin to brush my teeth black
like the three legged pot of clay?
tell me in the sound of your voice;
what does igqira mean when he says
"ukufa kuse mbizeni" *

* death is in the pot

Big brother

I still have to learn
the ways to become a fool –
to twist and break necks
of young daughters
and shout it loud with glee

Listen carefully big brother
to the rhythm of a fart
and savour the sound of the dumb –

I wish to have been born
by raped womb
and have artistic precision
to rape repeatedly the robust ones
with turbulent passion –
I could be that crazy

Unless
you exorcise
and silence the scream
of our sweet sisters
Unless
you exorcise the demon in me –
the poverty
that degrades and humiliates
my mind

for Titshalakazi

There's purity
in the presence of your
softness
and emptiness –
like the black sun
gazing proudly
over the meridian

like a doe,
I am imbued by pride
to have touched you
to have caressed you

Train-ride

Through a train window
I saw a tiny silver painted roof
in the midst of the forest

I opened the window
and the house seemed
to be moving
But it stayed the same
as if resisting the power
of the wounded forest

I wandered through my mind
searching the pain
of the forest, but I lost its track
on the rail lines

Rooihell

It drove me
into a total frenzy:
After the first admittance
as a gang member –
After I spilled the blood
of an innocent victim –
After the warders warmed me up
with their truncheons –
I was taken to single cells
(a section for violent inmates)

Life for the dwellers
followed a strict routine of
punctuated sound of doors
(that still grimaces me today)
being locked and unlocked
that made me feel
as if I'd slid into a run-down
parallel universe –
(especially in the early hours of the morning)

Spending my first
fright-filled night
in that claustrophobic
stink of stale urine
was like dying slowly from toes upwards

It was hell
down by the sea –
(I was in "rooi hell")

Your warm hands

Suddenly I find myself next to
your dark windows
of pain –
behind our secret smile

Joy has become our laughter
as our love
hangs up in the stars

Suddenly i find myself happy
for you –

Your warm hands
are constantly caressing the chain
so cold inside my soul

17/7728

steel doors widely
embraced him
(wide open)
ready to swallow
another pride of human kind –

deep in he dived
like a sardine
going for a swim
with sharks

the waters were wild
tuned in –
the waves rocked and rolled –
to the beat he danced
(so naive like a sheep lost in the wilderness
of jackals)

"Two-Two!! Fola!"
was his daily music
to be counted in and out his second life
(for he was just a statistic)

On the sunset side

She scratched and kicked
like a cross breed of a mule and
a tigress – he ripped her skirt off
and shredded her undergarments
until
her virginly breasts jutted
free and
with full force
her long tapering thighs stretched
and her bruised
buttocks spread wide open
and pressed
hard on rocky ground

he entered her
planting
the rotten seed –
salt tears burned her cheeks
and ran into the corners
of her mouth
like two tributaries of the
river of silence –
(she was in the pain-dream)
like ice she melted on his body
and clawed him
with her limp hands
conquered she was
and trembled like a hare that survived a chase
and her mound burned like furnace –
She wanted to run free.

Wrath

I say:
"every drop of my ink will curse
your balls"
And my children of my children
will know peace to mix not with your
progeny

In the tear of my eye
I swear:
"your pain will last a lifetime"
And your future
will be frozen like the waste lands

For you denied me a plate of food
in the days of endless agony!

Fantasy

You took off your panties
inside a scream
of my personal journal
to seduce my walls and chains

In your winter
you turned to me
to touch my sun
with your wet moonlips –
And your heart of passion
floated
inside my fucked up head

And the mound of your innocence
SWELLED
to the twisted horrors of
our burning lovemaking
as we coiled
and intertwined
on the bed of virginity
between the sheets of
Fantasy

And the love inside your
juicy pocket
became a memoir
for the lonely
poets
(who made love only to their poems)

Queen of queens

i curse the shrill
in our mad music, deep down the soul river –
in the name of the love goddess
and am spitting rage to the bled page
of lifeless moon and the stars –

in my demonic blood
i refuse to hide the truth of your smile
the beauty of your nature –
and am knocking at the doors of reality
with violent fists of conscience

your absence is tempting me to enter
into my dusty books
and stalk your past like a rabid rapist –
everywhere i look
i pray to master the technique and the spell

of returning you my love –
i shine my shrine with silver
and beat the drumsounds of Congo
to block the devils that crack the surface
of your coming home way

and i fast for your second coming
and dream of you as the queen of queens –
and i even map your thighs on a blank sheet
(and notice a little girl wearing her mother's bracelet)
and learn to kill the womb of despair.

Can we still...?

Can we still be friends
without me hurting you?
can we...
     hold on to the light of life
and let the music float
above the oceans...?

Can we still
             lose our eyes
for each other
             like we used to
without
       going blind?

Wednesday

(after Vallejo)

Once and no more
and never again
these words
will wipe away
these tears
like a white handkerchief

Once and no more
will this pain
crackle these armbones
full of good life
and bad news

And never again
will I sit under my shadow
just like today
this Wednesday –
even after so many words

Life is dead

(for the late Cynthia X. Mkrakra)

O life is dead
with your tender touch
that muses soft echoes.

And these cool waters
seem to dance
to the musical feast of the night
the night of solitude.

Hence these lonely winds
counting my blessings
leaf by leaf –
as they are shed off me
in this Autumn.

What will Spring be like?

Black silent tears

(from Prisoner 95595305, to Keabetsoe Tlale)

Inside the hut of my
memories –
At the black softness
of your laughter –
You blushed at the grey walls
Flirted with those
steel doors. And smiled

at their iron keys
until the wings of pain
carried you
to a lake of tears –
Your black silent tears.

Robber's confession

It was the empty cupboard
at home
that made me do it –
I could not help it
when I looked at my mama's dry face
and cracked lips –
like a parched field –
her withered hands
tortured my vision.

I would not allow my sister
to peddle her greasy hole
to put food on the table
to humiliate my manhood
(my family's pride)
the blood I bled.

Though I will never again
I am telling you:
the tattered rags that we wore
the fragile voice
of my mother's cry at prayer times
the moonless nights
of our home with no candle
made me do it.

Even my friends say
no one sane would have done that:
Forgetting that an empty stomach
is insensitive and wild.

Whispering promise

along the evolutionary road
i was frightened
by the blackness of my shadow –
i looked into the faceless
cowl of the night
and ghosts rode the wind
and echoes of past applause
froze into the air
between the black trees
of the eternal pilgrim

and i heard my voice,
like the sound of frosty falling leaves –
inviting me to a stroll
up the avenue of dreams

When she cried

To you I lacked all reasons
as if made of wax
my smile was guilt
and my scent a sin
You never presented me with flowers
but thistles and prickly pears

Nevertheless,
for you I did care through
a road
as empty and endless like a day
without bread –
yet you could not even imagine
the days of someone condemned to love:

That's what she said
when she cried

Zukiswa's song

When we met I was a virginly pride
to the people of my village –
a flora
that smelled all seasons
(a symbol of peace)

Gentleman
you broke my father's kraal –
and promised me the world

Now, like a flower
I am slowly withering –
but you are gone with your
honey suckle smile –

I am no longer your milk gourd
for you drink in well crafted
calabashes –
while I drink in a lake of tears.

In the last flicker of light

(for Small, who died of HIV/Aids
in Prison Hospital 2002)

It was after twelve midnight.
I know because it was after
the second round of the second
night watch. Inmates were asleep.

They came with a knife made of
steel spoon, thrusted it into my throat –
And I was told to be silent.
They undressed me
and penetrated my anus-hole.
As they pounded over me
torment filled my soul
and I wanted to die
for my manhood was denied
and my dignity shattered into pieces
(It was my first experience of prison life)

The pain of darkness
confusion and fear
immobilised my mind
And despair flooded me, as I lay there
in hell alone, after what felt like eternity –
Trembling
I got up and dressed.

I had flash-backs of them
thrusting and thrusting
as if boring a hole in my soul –
as I recalled one of them saying:

"My Rosie, my baby" –
That was my burden to carry alone
I sadly thought –
As fear set in, recalling what one
of them said: "Speak of this to anyone,
then you die boy"
My eyes were burning
and I felt tears pricking
my eyelashes
And I stormed like a lightning
into the shower.

Cold water pounded onto my skin
as if laughing my shame –
no soap no water
could wash away the dirt
I felt inside.

That's all he told me
lying there on that bed
ready for his demise –
to meet his Maker.

Avenues of my soul

Between the spirit of the age
And the darkness of rage
lies the angel of the pen
who writes the stories of men
inside the depths of the black hole
in the avenues of my soul.

Yet I read the rotten page
of the black man's heritage
But there is nothing to learn
as it comes from the mind of white men
I swear I will not trouble the hole
in the black avenues of my soul.

Oh learned men who never learned
how to be proud countrymen
Swaggering pride of song and fight
A world unconquerable by white
Magic sorrows from the black hole
in the avenues of my soul.

The protest that I tried to stage
Was it not good for this time and age?
Gently replied the Angel of my pen
"Ask not from your countrymen.
Go to the depths of the black hole
and ask the avenues of your soul."

they wait in dark places
jagged surfaces
and blunt edges –
behind fences and sentries,

Straight talk

my little boy asked
one day

Father
did you bring me here
so that I can talk too much
and be lost
inside the forest of my words? –

and I replied
to him

As for me
love was never the word
and by mistake you were born –
It all started
after the party and booze –
It's no wonder
your prattle is like music out of tune
to my ears

iindlavini

they wait in dark places
jagged surfaces
and blunt edges –
behind fences and sentries,
like a doomsday weapon
too dangerous to touch

they walk and talk
with images of pain contained
in their memory
like a song whose melody
you cannot sing –
death written in their faces
as they duck
their mother's kisses

The 19:30 Man

A dead silence fell
between us in the cell
like the passing of an angel –

In that house of aborted hopes I saw death
gliding like a serpent,
and felt the leprous stench reeking

I felt dirty of grime
and wanted an ablution
to cleanse me of
my sin and crime –

Half past seven!
there was sullen gloom
in that death room.

I knew we were doomed
when my food turned bitter
and lost its appetizing
(Gabriel came upon him)

Like fog invading the mountains
I saw death attacking our cell
it was 19:30
The Simunye clock struck for news

as if it knew
we had sad news –
(We lost a man)

Song from the grass

hope has become our communal graves
(in this train)
in this memory of the chain
hanging up mast high
to mock the fallen and forgotten braves –
(to celebrate this lie)

yet we don the lice infested outfit
of obedience traded and sold
for silk and gold –
and still in the texture of this dream we hide
with our toyi toyi worn·out feet
to announce the curse of our black pride

is it true, when two bulls meet
only the grass suffers defeat?

Free at last

(to the memory of an inmate
who died at the single cells)

he tripped and crashed on concrete –
his heart swelled
with a vibrating noise
head on cement –
his wish
(to wake from the nightmare)

it was after a finished work
(and he seemed lifeless to them)
and they stood on
brandishing their truncheons
(two ruffians)
he looked up and succumbed again
to the unappreciated luxury of his sleep

coldness embraced him
and darkness witnessed it all
and the wind sang a mournful hymn
(as they choked in pleasure and relief)

Rhythm of ignorance

You shouted happiness
through the gaps of this pain –
and the comfortlessness of my skin
screamed in response

Your hunger demanded
my forbidden zone
in a conjugal manner

Instead I wanted you to know
my status
I wanted you to hear the language
of desire
in its miserable form
But...
you reasoned with excuses
so suicidal for a reason

as you pulled down the cotton
from your pubic haired mound
pleading to burn with me,

before I could utter a No!
your fingers closed my lips
with their wet nakedness
And that other odour
screamed "The door is open"
And our breathing became a rhythm
of our ignorance –
An end to your innocence.

Angel eyes of the wind

(letter to a dead lover)

You once called me
Angel eyes of the wind
with the deep melody of your voice
whose blood has ceased to be –
Strange, though
I no longer grieve for you
But
I still find the tone of
your voice
that keeps telling me
I am alone.

We both know that
I sired from you a flower
a Primrose –
Sometimes to me you seem near
Perhaps it is because of her
Somehow I wish
you could enter her dreams
and your sister's dreams
tell them the truth
the paternal truth –
(Pardon me for that)

With a resemblance like yours
I cannot help but smile
whenever I pass by her
She has grown into a woman now
and that makes me want to hear her say:

"Papa" till the end of days.
For I am alone
And since your unannounced parting
There is no womb
willing to swallow my sperm
It seems as if the angels of fertility
have cursed me.

I wanted to die last night

I wanted to die last night
after the morning call
after you cried –
after the last watch's rounds
I took a sheet tore it into strips
made a noose
like the "Laksman" did

Wenzani?
that voice broke the silence of my demise
and returned me back to midnight blues
silent and shocked
I tried to tie the knot
But...
their iron keys penetrated the hole
of that steel door
piercing my ears with that eerie sound
of iron kissing steel –
My mind raced back to reality
And I felt a lump in my throat
But I didn't cry
For I wanted to die

They took and put me
in a straightjacket
and brought a shrink
to shrink my mind
But...
her voice was soft like yours
And tears flooded my conscience –
And, oh for you I wanted to die!

Harvest

an old lady
with grey hair
standing barefooted
in a backyard garden
holding a robust cabbage
smile lighting her face
as if saying:
"this is a crowning glory
a celebration of my toil"
and i felt good
and satisfied just like black soil.

I have lost myself

I have lost myself
in the thoughts about you
And you seemed to be far away alone –
And I forgot to remember
the help and the love of ALLAH
because of you.

I have lost myself and kept on wandering
inside the sound of your voice
that reverberated
like the last echo in my mind
And I forgot to dress like a man
for your love
made me feel like a small boy.

Melancholy

Lying there in the dark
Doors and windows open
Listening   smoking
Deeper and deeper

You smacking the air
You digging your fists in –
(You holding my hands)

And for the first time
I feel the condition
Of being human
I feel the ache

And my soul longs to sing
In a thousand secret whispers
A song
To all the sad people in the world.

Prayer-song

I have become one
with the chain gangs
and prison
belongs to my name –
though I belong to the best
of your creation.

Orange and black
have become threads
that weave my life
with their round articulation –
And dogs guard me
when I eat
by way of punishment.
I am a cow dung
to my people.

God, my good Lord:
I do not know which name
is suitable for me to call you
so that you can hear –
Perhaps Qamata like my ancestors did
or Jehovah as the Jews and Christians do
Maybe Allah like the Arabs do
But whatever
You are the Master of Creation.

Lord of creation again I call to you
I call for you
to help me from the demon of pain
I call for you to adorn me
with love and truth

with love and truth
I call for you to give me a second chance
and save me
from my wretchedness.

Oh, Allah
with these tears to you I pray
between phases of time
and trembling impassionate lips
I pray for you
to define for me the straight path
and let me not be
one of the inheritors of your wrath.
Take away the roundness
of my tongue,
and my fleeting desires for street life
'cause I want to be next to you.
Give me time to recover
in a big space
in the free world.

I know my fellow human-beings
might not want to forgive me
but Lord
only you can forgive me –
I have tried to forgive myself
but I just come from hell and back
it seems I am wandering to nowhere.

The anger in me Lord
keeps me in chains –
my presence has become a shadow
and future beckons me
like a laughing grave –

like a laughing grave –
oh please Lord help me to survive
the agony within me.

Home

Out of dirt and dust
at the street corner
lies a semi-painted structure
of cement –
only four rooms –
a bitterness and hurt
that hardens my heart

Inside the poverty-
stricken souls
under the roof with
sorrow filled holes –
after the common scream
of the gate's rusty hinges –
a creaking wooden floor
welcomes you home
to come brew fresh hopes
after a choked and narrow day
that laments hardship
for a surviving poet.

Spirit of the morning

As I trod in solitude
with the bleeding
feet of my heart
on a thorny wilderness
of agony's afterdays

As life was Autumn
that filled my soul with leaves
of despair –
Sunshine came like
the spirit of the morning.

And in its sound
I knew, at last I found
the oasis of mystery
In the desert of my existence.

i lost a poem

i will never be happy
till i find the poem
that i lost –
the poem of how i loved you
how i loved the way
we kissed
on our first day

When I come out

I will undoubtedly lick
the peanut hue of your nipples
and search for the rose in the garden
below your navel

When I come out from this cold

I will be a demon let loose
to explore the landscapes
of your bare soul
and your desert·like body